PIANO SOLO

DOWNTON ABBEY

MUSIC FROM THE
MOTION PICTURE SOUNDTRACK

ISBN 978-1-5400-7068-5

For all works contained herein:
Unauthorized copying, arranging, adapting, recording, Internet posting, public performance,
or other distribution of the music in this publication is an infringement of copyright.
Infringers are liable under the law.

Visit Hal Leonard Online at
www.halleonard.com

Contact us:
Hal Leonard
7777 West Bluemound Road
Milwaukee, WI 53213
Email: info@halleonard.com

In Europe, contact:
Hal Leonard Europe Limited
42 Wigmore Street
Marylebone, London, W1U 2RN
Email: info@halleonardeurope.com

In Australia, contact:
Hal Leonard Australia Pty. Ltd.
4 Lentara Court
Cheltenham, Victoria, 3192 Australia
Email: info@halleonard.com.au

A ROYAL COMMAND

By JOHN LAWRENCE LUNN

Moderately

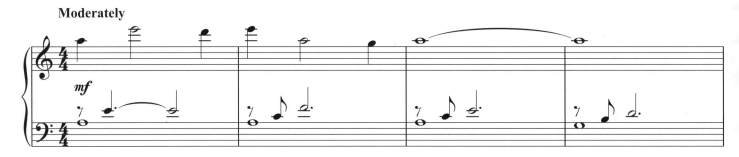

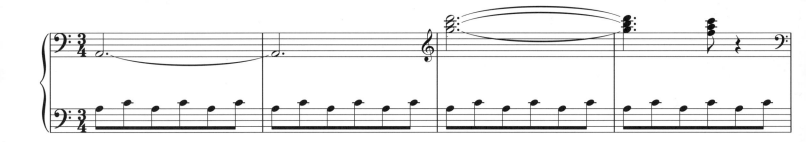

Copyright © 2019 DEPOTSOUND LTD. and DU VINAGE PUBLISHING LTD.
All Rights for DEPOTSOUND LTD. Administered by UNIVERSAL - POLYGRAM INTERNATIONAL PUBLISHING, INC.
All Rights Reserved   Used by Permission

3

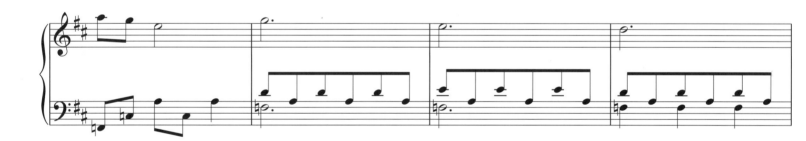

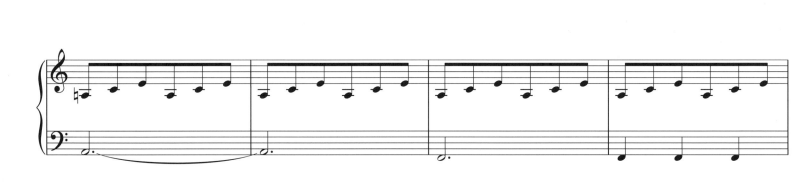

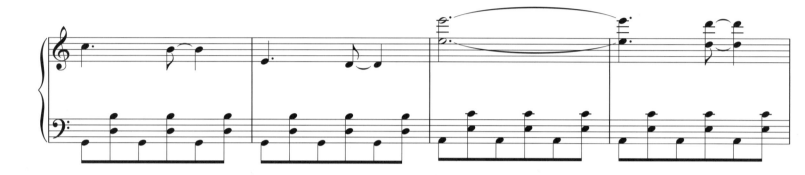

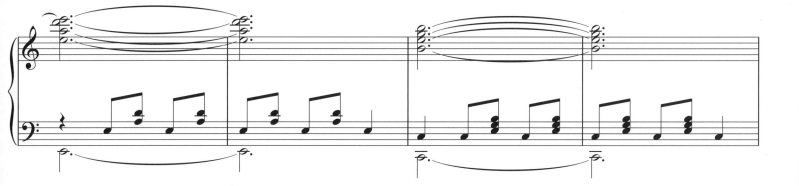

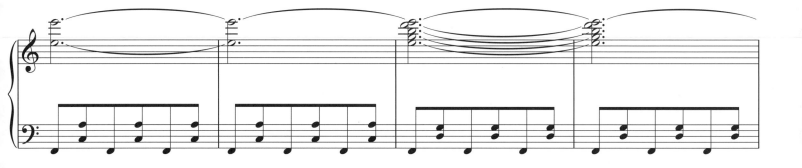

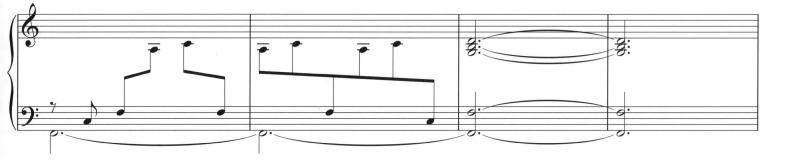

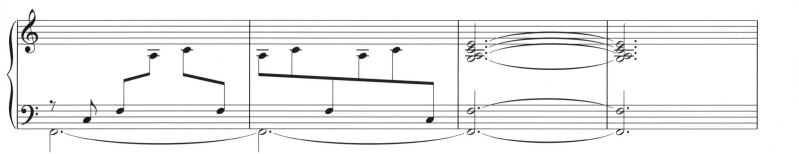

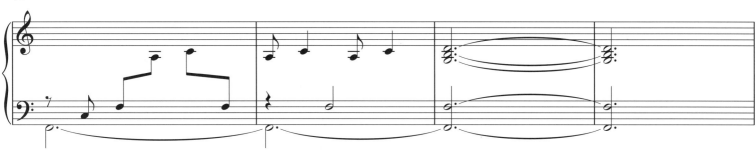

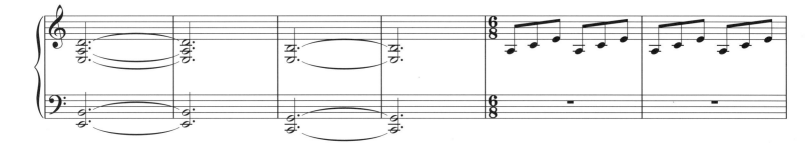

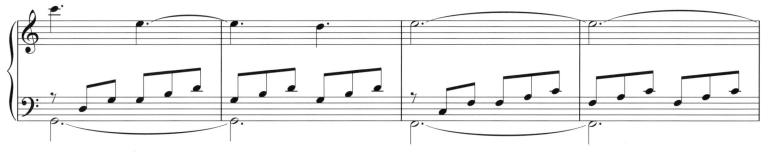

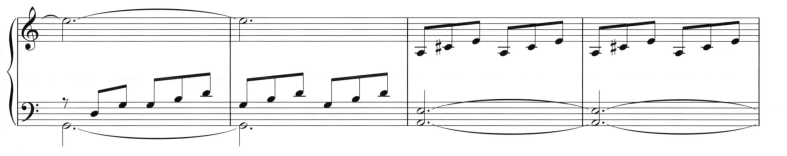

GLEAM AND SPARKLE

By JOHN LAWRENCE LUNN

Moderately fast

Pedal ad lib. throughout

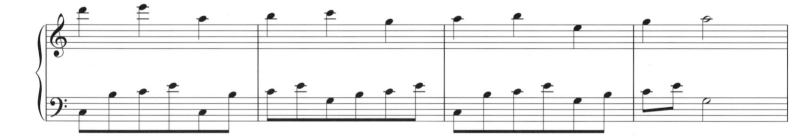

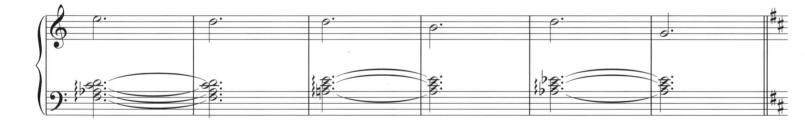

Copyright © 2019 CARNIVAL FILM AND TELEVISION LIMITED, FOCUS-GRAMERCY MUSIC and DU VINAGE PUBLISHING LTD.
All Rights for CARNIVAL FILM AND TELEVISION LIMITED Administered by UNIVERSAL - POLYGRAM INTERNATIONAL PUBLISHING, INC.
All Rights for FOCUS-GRAMERCY MUSIC Administered by UNIVERSAL MUSIC CORP.
All Rights for DU VINAGE PUBLISHING LTD. in the U.S. Administered by R3D MUSIC
All Rights Reserved   Used by Permission

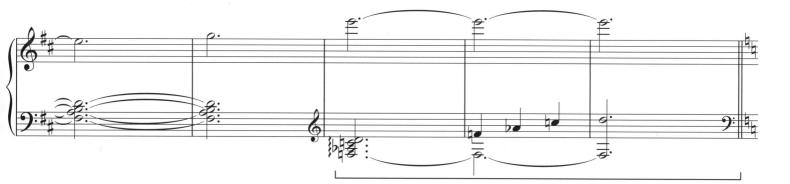

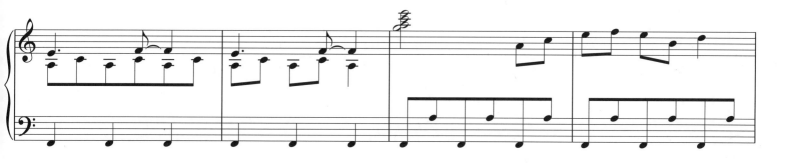
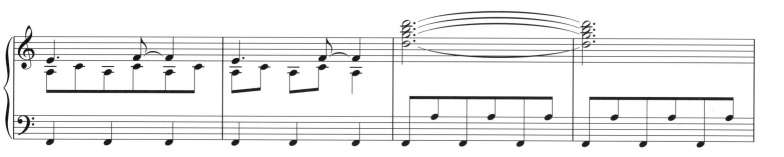

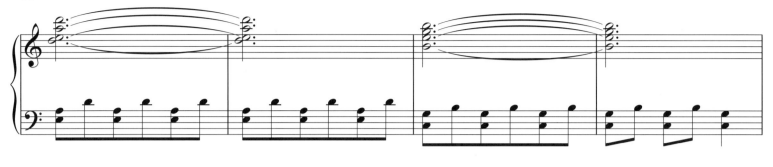

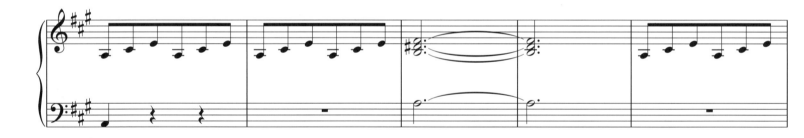

Moderately, expressively

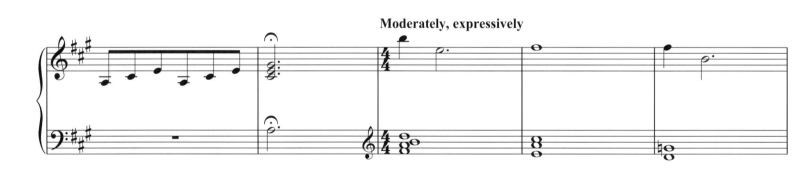

accel.

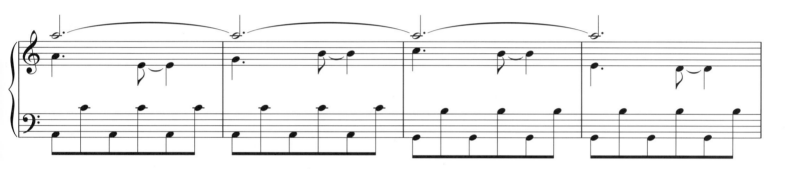

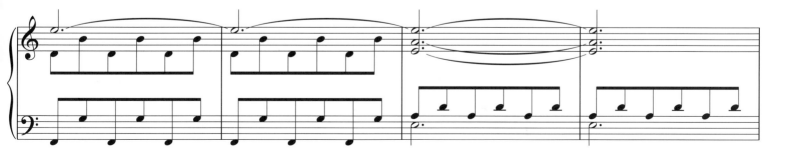

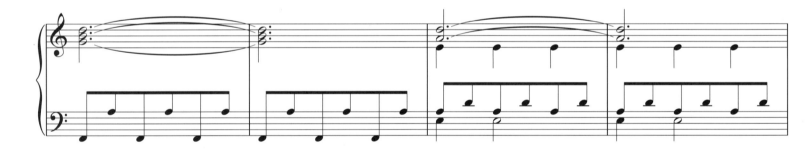

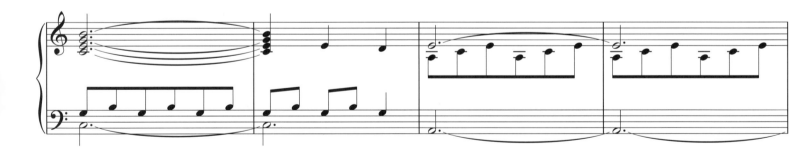

GOD IS A MONARCHIST

By JOHN LAWRENCE LUNN

Moderately fast

Copyright © 2019 DEPOTSOUND LTD. and DU VINAGE PUBLISHING LTD.
All Rights for DEPOTSOUND LTD. Administered by UNIVERSAL - POLYGRAM INTERNATIONAL PUBLISHING, INC.
All Rights Reserved   Used by Permission

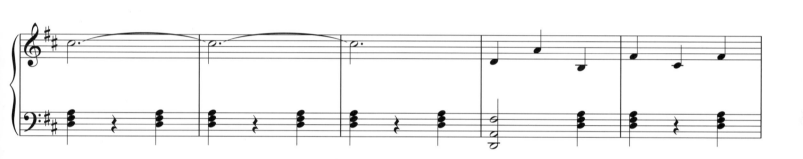

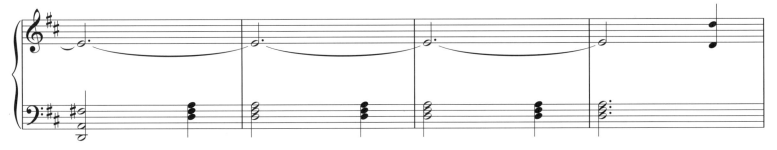

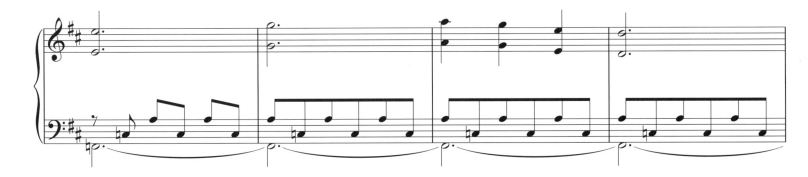

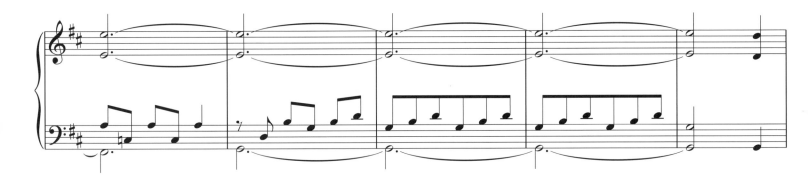

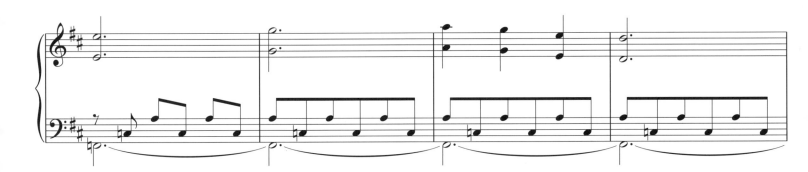

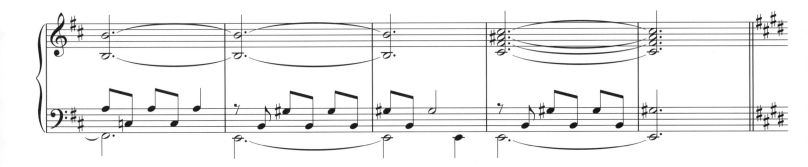

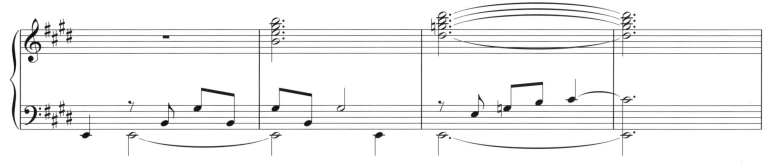

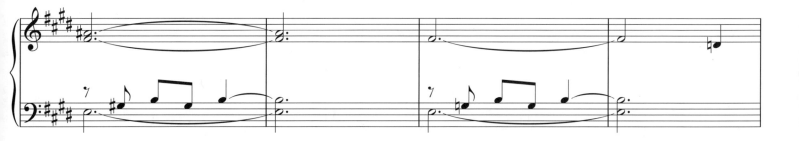

MAUD

By JOHN LAWRENCE LUNN

Moderately slow, expressively

Pedal ad lib. throughout

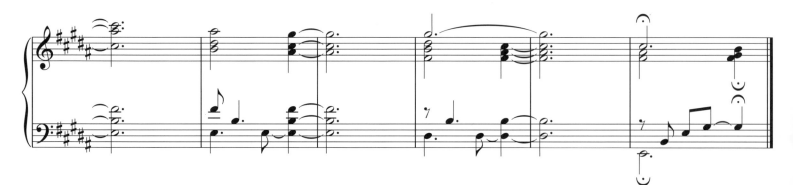

Copyright © 2019 FOCUS-GRAMERCY MUSIC and DU VINAGE PUBLISHING LTD.
All Rights for FOCUS-GRAMERCY MUSIC Administered by UNIVERSAL MUSIC CORP.
All Rights for DU VINAGE PUBLISHING LTD. in the U.S. Administered by R3D MUSIC
All Rights Reserved   Used by Permission

HONOUR RESTORED

By JOHN LAWRENCE LUNN

Copyright © 2019 CARNIVAL FILM AND TELEVISION LIMITED, FOCUS-GRAMERCY MUSIC and DU VINAGE PUBLISHING LTD.
All Rights for CARNIVAL FILM AND TELEVISION LIMITED Administered by UNIVERSAL - POLYGRAM INTERNATIONAL PUBLISHING, INC.
All Rights for FOCUS-GRAMERCY MUSIC Administered by UNIVERSAL MUSIC CORP.
All Rights for DU VINAGE PUBLISHING LTD. in the U.S. Administered by R3D MUSIC
All Rights Reserved   Used by Permission

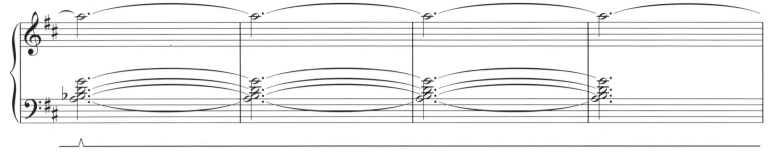

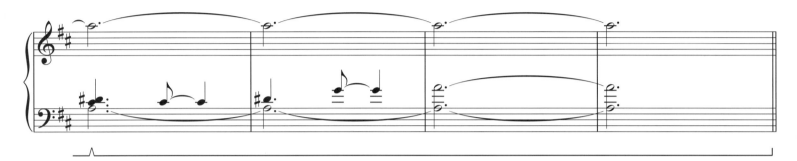

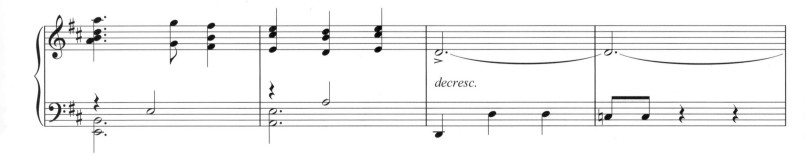

NEVER SEEN ANYTHING LIKE IT

By JOHN LAWRENCE LUNN
and CHRISTOPHER MARCUS EGAN

Copyright © 2019 FOCUS-GRAMERCY MUSIC and DU VINAGE PUBLISHING LTD.
All Rights for FOCUS-GRAMERCY MUSIC Administered by UNIVERSAL MUSIC CORP.
All Rights for DU VINAGE PUBLISHING LTD. in the U.S. Administered by R3D MUSIC
All Rights Reserved   Used by Permission

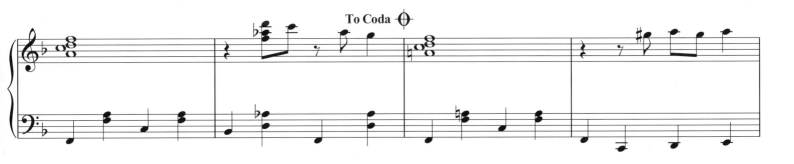

To Coda

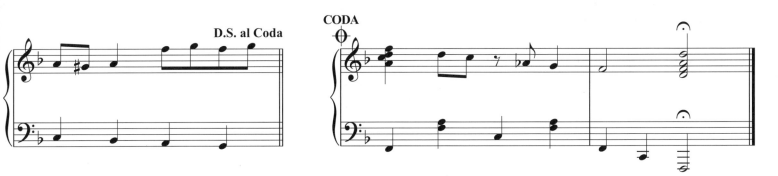

TAKING LEAVE

By JOHN LAWRENCE LUNN

Moderately slow

Moderately fast

Copyright © 2019 FOCUS-GRAMERCY MUSIC and DU VINAGE PUBLISHING LTD.
All Rights for FOCUS-GRAMERCY MUSIC Administered by UNIVERSAL MUSIC CORP.
All Rights for DU VINAGE PUBLISHING LTD. in the U.S. Administered by R3D MUSIC
All Rights Reserved   Used by Permission

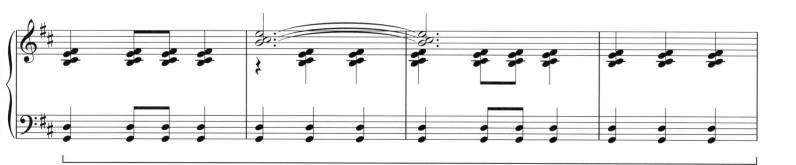

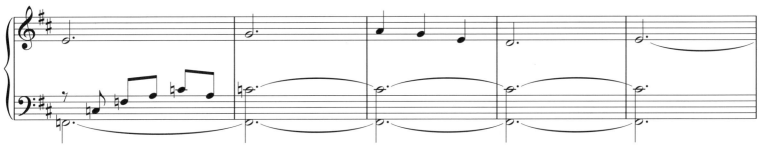

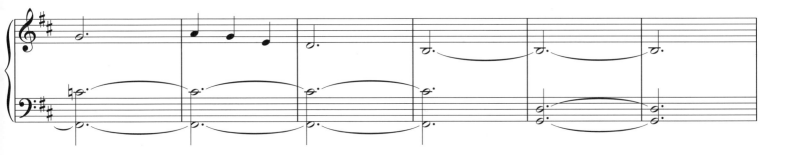

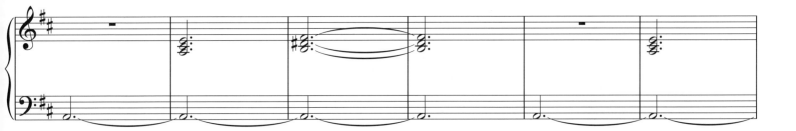

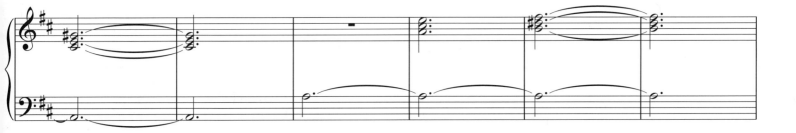

YOU ARE THE BEST OF ME

By JOHN LAWRENCE LUNN

Copyright © 2019 DEPOTSOUND LTD. and DU VINAGE PUBLISHING LTD.
All Rights for DEPOTSOUND LTD. Administered by UNIVERSAL - POLYGRAM INTERNATIONAL PUBLISHING, INC.
All Rights Reserved   Used by Permission

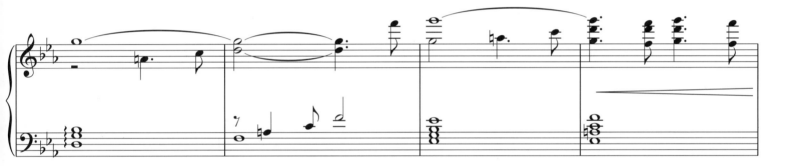

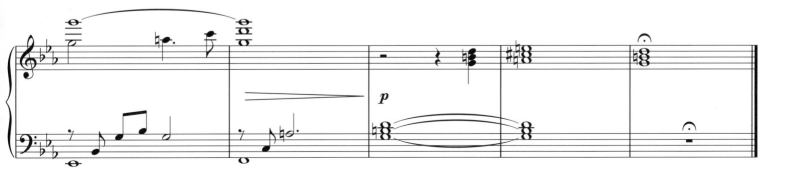

SUNSET WALTZ

By JOHN LAWRENCE LUNN,
ALASTAIR JOHN KING and DP

Moderately fast

Copyright © 2019 FOCUS-GRAMERCY MUSIC and DU VINAGE PUBLISHING LTD.
All Rights for FOCUS-GRAMERCY MUSIC Administered by UNIVERSAL MUSIC CORP.
All Rights for DU VINAGE PUBLISHING LTD. in the U.S. Administered by R3D MUSIC
All Rights Reserved   Used by Permission

38

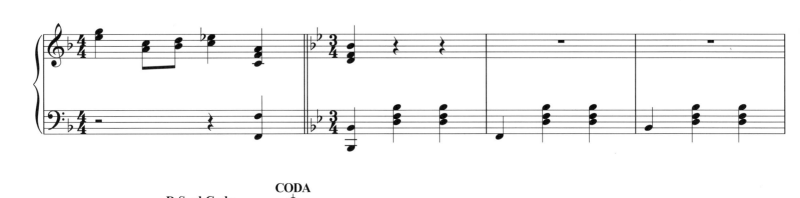

D.S. al Coda

CODA

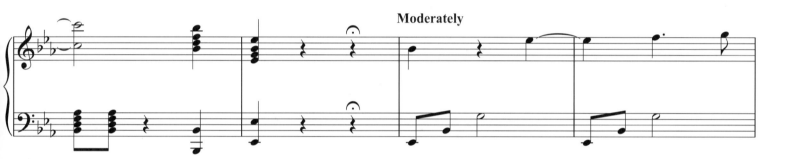

Moderately

40

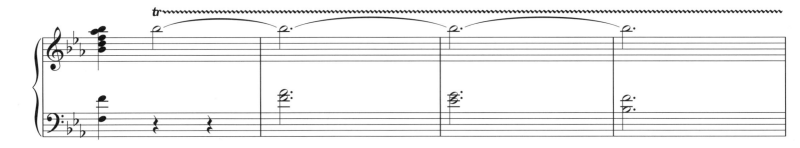

ONE HUNDRED YEARS OF DOWNTON

By JOHN LAWRENCE LUNN

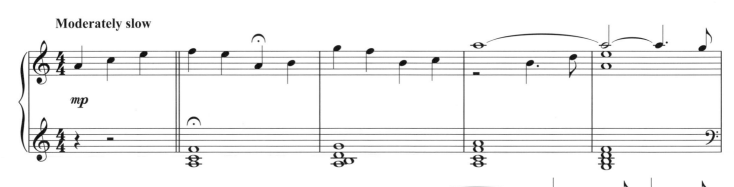

Copyright © 2019 CARNIVAL FILM AND TELEVISION LIMITED, FOCUS-GRAMERCY MUSIC and DU VINAGE PUBLISHING LTD.
All Rights for CARNIVAL FILM AND TELEVISION LIMITED Administered by UNIVERSAL - POLYGRAM INTERNATIONAL PUBLISHING, INC.
All Rights for FOCUS-GRAMERCY MUSIC Administered by UNIVERSAL MUSIC CORP.
All Rights for DU VINAGE PUBLISHING LTD. in the U.S. Administered by R3D MUSIC
All Rights Reserved   Used by Permission

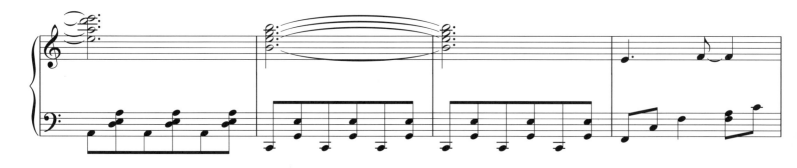

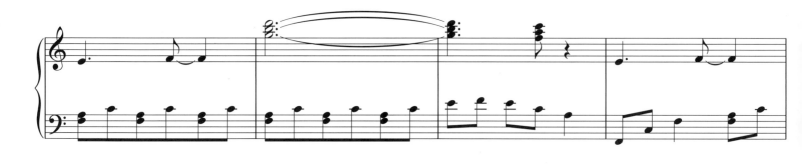

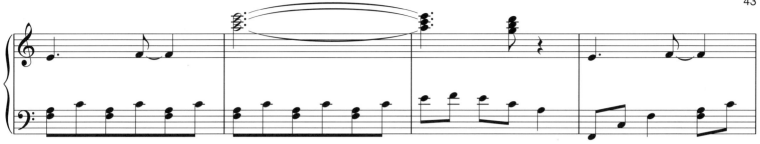

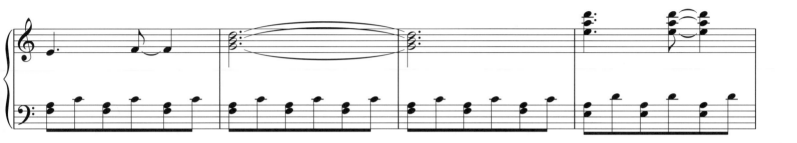

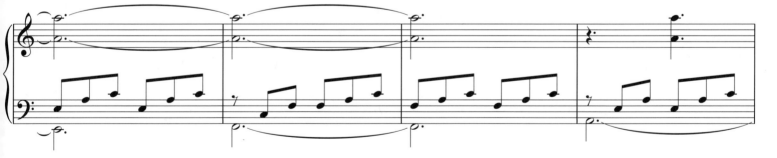

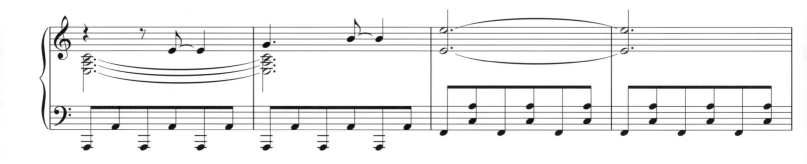

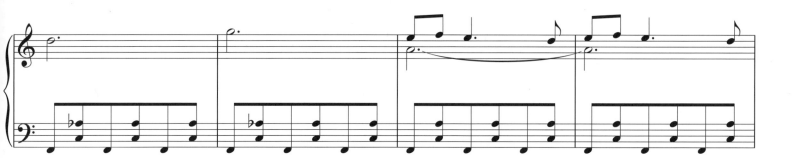

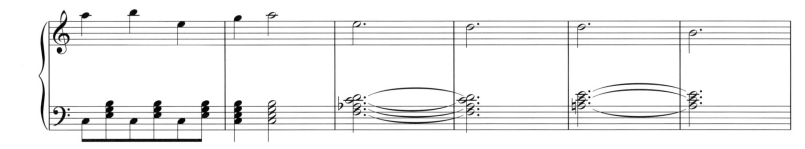

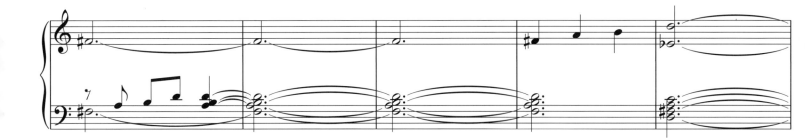

Slowly, expressively

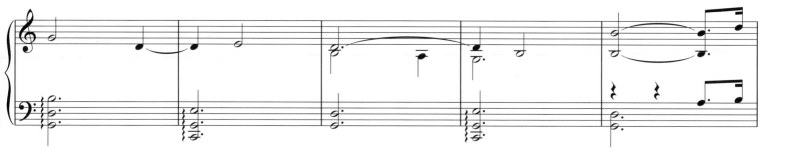

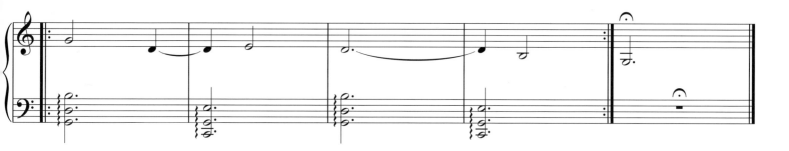